Digital Commerce Strategies

Your Online Guidebook to Increasing Sales Funnel Success

George L. Geyer

Table of Content

Introduction

Chapter One

The Basis for Online Success

Chapter Two

Crafting an Irresistible Offer

Chapter Three

Funnelology: The Art of Sales Funnels

Chapter Four

Mastering Traffic Generation

Chapter Five

Understanding and Taking Care of Your Audience

Chapter 6

The Secrets of Sales Copywriting

Chapter Seven

Improving Conversion Rates

Chapter Eight

The Role of Value Ladders

Chapter Nine

Traffic Temperature and Segmentation

Chapter Ten

The Strength of Follow-Up Funnels

Chapter Eleven

Webinar Funnels' Secrets

Chapter Twelve

Building Effective Membership Sites

Chapter Thirteen
The Digital Commerce Strategies Toolbox
Chapter Fourteen
Scaling Your Online Empire
Chapter Fithteen
Leaving a Legacy and Volunteering
Conclusion

Introduction

In the dimly lit workplace, Sarah glanced at her computer screen, thinking about the tremendous issue that lay before her. She had been tasked with driving a key project for her organisation, one that needed navigating through new realms of technical innovation. The goal at hand was to revamp their main product, a venture that requires an unprecedented degree of innovation and competence.

Drawing upon the pooled expertise of her team, Sarah methodically produced a roadmap for the project. Each facet was thoroughly researched, dissected, and optimised. The team's collaborative brainstorming sessions resembled a symphony of ideas, seamlessly weaving together unique thoughts that pushed the limits of what was considered feasible.

As the project advanced, new problems developed, threatening to derail their progress. Sarah's leadership talents emerged as she adeptly navigated her team through these perilous seas. She fostered open communication, producing an atmosphere where setbacks were recognized as chances for progress.

Months passed, and the project reached completion. Sarah and her team had expertly navigated through a maze of technological complexity, emerging on the other side with a new solution that promised to transform their sector. The unknown route they had walked had led to innovation, and their united efforts had opened the way for a better future.

With their eyes focused firmly on the horizon, Sarah and her crew began on the next chapter of their adventure, armed with the certainty that they could conquer any lay ahead.

In the relentless, ever-evolving terrain of the digital sphere, where the internet meets business, lies a dense tapestry of techniques and secrets that, when mastered, may unleash incredible success. "Digital Commerce Strategies
" is a detailed examination of the key concepts and covert procedures that drive the victory of internet firms. As companies rapidly pivot towards the virtual arena, it becomes necessary to grasp the cryptic algorithms of e-commerce, and this book acts as your guide.

In the first chapter, we construct the foundation upon which online success is based, anchoring our knowledge in the subtleties of the digital environment. The ensuing chapters dive into the skill of generating attractive offers, navigating the complicated network of sales funnels, and the expertise of traffic generation—each part being a vital component in the battle for digital dominance.

Moreover, we explore the intricate architecture of audience engagement, showing the road to cultivating a loyal following via successful email marketing, content tactics, and targeted communications. Sales copywriting, the quiet power behind conversions, is disclosed, supported by the approach of conversion rate optimization.

The book goes on to disclose the secrets of value ladders, traffic segmentation, and the power of follow-up funnels. Along the way, we expose the possibilities of webinar funnels and the art of developing high-performing membership sites. In the latter chapters, we offer the crucial toolset of internet marketing, tactics for growing, and the important ideas of legacy-building and giving back.

In the quest for greatness inside the digital domain, "Digital Commerce Strategies

" is your definitive guide, precisely constructed to light the path, uncovering the enigmatic tactics that allow people and organisations to prosper in the digital era.

Chapter One

The Basis for Online Success

1.1 Recognizing the Digital Environment

A thorough understanding of the digital world is a crucial prerequisite for online success in the relentlessly evolving contemporary corporate scene. Businesses congregate in the digital terrain, which has many sides and fluid dynamics, to engage with, enthral, and eventually convert their audience. The digital ecosystem is supported by a variety of social media platforms, search engines, e-commerce websites, and developing technologies, all of which are constantly evolving. Understanding the subtleties of customer behaviour, technical changes, and the competitive environment is crucial for navigating this complex environment.

1.2 The Influence of Online Marketing

The power of Internet marketing cannot be emphasised when information availability and connection are defining characteristics. It is the ideal method for reaching a large worldwide audience with your brand's message, goods, and services with unmatched accuracy and reach. Online marketing includes a wide range of tactics and platforms, from social media marketing, content development, and email campaigns to search engine optimization (SEO), pay-per-click advertising (PPC), and SEO. Online marketing's strength is in its capacity to customise messages, target certain demographics, analyse data, and adjust plans in real-time, maximising your online presence and enhancing the effect of your brand.

1.3 The Framework for Digital Commerce Strategies

The Digital Commerce Strategies
Framework, a tactical guide that has helped numerous online business owners succeed in the digital sphere, is at the core of this book. This framework combines tried-and-true ideas with novel approaches and cutting-edge methods that have been successful in generating online riches. It is a framework that is based on the principles of creating alluring offers, creating efficient sales funnels, mastering traffic generation, and cultivating a devoted client base. The Digital Commerce Strategies
Framework goes beyond simple theory by providing practical advice and a methodical method for converting digital promise into observable success.

1.4 Choosing Your Online Objectives

Any online project must begin with a list of goals that are precise and well-defined. Your online objectives serve as both a purpose and a compass for your digital journey. To set these objectives, you must carefully consider what you want to accomplish—whether it's more sales, more brand recognition, more leads, or more satisfied clients. Goals should also be SMART, precise, measurable, achievable, relevant, and time-limited. They act as the benchmark by which advancements may be assessed and tactics improved. Setting compelling and clear online objectives is the first step in laying a solid foundation for your success online in the fluid and dynamic world of the digital environment.

Chapter Two

Crafting an Irresistible Offer

2.1 The Importance of an Offer

In the ever-evolving digital market, the cornerstone of successful online initiatives depends upon the establishment of a compelling proposition. It acts as the first point of contact between your organisation and the prospective consumer, functioning as a compelling invitation to interact. A successful offer goes beyond a basic product or service; it answers the fundamental issue of "What's in it for the customer?" By concentrating on this essential question, you build the framework for developing a beneficial relationship with your audience.

2.2 Identifying Your Target Audience

Before developing an offer that connects, it is necessary to obtain a comprehensive knowledge of your target demographic. Identifying their individual requirements, interests, pain areas, and preferences is key to designing an offer that speaks directly to them. This entails detailed market research, segmentation, and personal construction. The more accurate and detailed your understanding of your target, the more effectively you can address their individual needs, boosting the chance of engagement and conversion.

2.3 Creating Value-Driven Offers

Creating deals that engage with your audience depends on the delivery of meaningful value. Value is the money of the digital environment, and it may emerge in numerous ways, such as cost savings, convenience, education, or amusement. Crafting value-driven products involves a careful balance between satisfying client requirements and exceeding their expectations. The objective is to create a solution or experience that not only satisfies their immediate needs but also leaves a lasting impact, creating trust and loyalty.

2.4 Testing and Optimising Your Offers

In the changing world of internet marketing, a set-it-and-forget-it attitude to offerings is ill-advised. Continuous progress is the watchword. Testing and optimization are the twin engines that produce sustained success. A/B testing, multivariate testing, and other data-driven tactics enable you to adjust your offerings based on real-time feedback. Analysing conversion rates, click-through rates, and client feedback helps you fine-tune your products, ensuring they stay relevant and attractive in a constantly evolving digital market. The iterative process of testing and improving your offerings is the foundation of a profitable internet company.

Chapter Three

Funnelology: The Art of Sales Funnels

3.1 Introduction to Sales Funnels

Sales funnels are the backbone of effective Internet marketing and sales initiatives. In this chapter, we look into the underlying ideas that support the notion of sales funnels. A sales funnel is simply a graphic depiction of the customer journey from first awareness to conversion. It's an organised process that walks prospects through multiple phases, each aimed to drive them closer to completing a purchase or doing a desired action.

Understanding the relevance of sales funnels is vital for every digital marketer or online company owner. It gives a methodical strategy for lead generation, nurturing, and conversion. Sales funnels help you plan out and improve every touchpoint of your customer's engagement with your brand, making your marketing activities more efficient and successful.

3.2 Building Effective Sales Funnels

Creating a successful sales funnel entails a laborious process that demands careful preparation and execution. It starts with a thorough grasp of your target audience and their demands. By recognizing their pain spots and desires, you can develop compelling offers and communications that appeal to them.

A well-structured sales funnel often comprises numerous phases, including awareness, interest, consideration, and conversion. Each stage has a distinct function, and it's crucial to customise your content and strategy appropriately. Moreover, the design and style of your funnel, together with the usage of compelling components like calls-to-action and scarcity strategies, play a key part in leading prospects through the funnel efficiently.

3.3 Funnel Hacking: Analysing Competitors

The notion of "funnel hacking" entails examining and evaluating the techniques implemented by rivals or successful organisations in your industry. This approach may give useful insights into what works and what doesn't. By studying the sales funnels of others, you may obtain a greater insight into their client acquisition and retention tactics.

Competitor analysis may help you uncover weaknesses in their strategy that you can exploit, as well as areas where you can distinguish yourself. It's a deliberate method of learning from people who have previously achieved success in your industry. This chapter will discuss the approaches and tools available for successful funnel hacking, helping you to obtain a competitive advantage in your business.

3.4 Conversion Optimization Strategies

In the realm of Internet marketing, conversion is the ultimate aim. However, attaining high conversion rates throughout your sales funnels might be tough. In this part, we investigate the art of conversion rate optimization (CRO). CRO comprises a methodical strategy to enhance the performance of your funnels by evaluating data, testing new features, and making data-driven choices.

We'll go into the significance of A/B testing, where you compare several versions of your funnel to discover which one works better. Additionally, we'll cover the psychological factors underlying great conversion methods, such as social proof, scarcity, and urgency. By applying established CRO tactics, you may enhance the effectiveness of your sales funnels, eventually leading to higher revenue and a more profitable online company.

Chapter Four

Mastering Traffic Generation

In the field of internet companies, traffic acts as the necessary lifeblood, the driving force that feeds the engine of success. Within this chapter, we dig into the subtleties of traffic creation, shining light on its crucial significance and the various techniques available for harnessing it successfully.

4.1 The Lifeblood of Your Online Business

Traffic, in its different forms, is the lifeblood of every internet firm. It reflects the flood of visitors to your digital domain, prospective consumers who examine your products, connect with your content, and, hopefully, convert into paying patrons. Without a consistent influx of visitors, even the most painstakingly created goods and services stay buried in the enormous expanse of the internet. Recognizing this, the first portion of this chapter underlines the vital role that traffic plays in the online business scene. It serves as the core principle that underlies all following talks on traffic creation tactics.

4.2 Organic vs. Paid Traffic

In the field of traffic creation, two key pathways lure entrepreneurs: organic and sponsored traffic. Each path has its particular traits, benefits, and obstacles. The second half of this chapter dissects these two techniques, giving a complete contrast that empowers you with the information to make educated selections. Organic traffic comprises enhancing your digital assets to organically attract users, employing tactics like search engine optimization (SEO) and content marketing. Conversely, sponsored traffic depends on advertising and promotions, delivering rapid exposure in return for monetary investment. Understanding the differences between these channels is crucial for adapting your traffic generation plan to line with your company goals.

4.3 SEO Strategies for Traffic Growth

Among the pantheon of organic traffic creation approaches, search engine optimization (SEO) ranks as a cornerstone. It is the art and science of increasing your online presence to gain better ranks in search engine results pages (SERPs). This third segment digs into the complexities of SEO, including insights into keyword research, on-page and off-page optimization approaches, and the significance of remaining alert to ever-evolving search engine algorithms. By understanding SEO tactics, you may unleash persistent, free traffic that flows from search engines, bringing your digital assets before people actively search for your goods or services.

4.4 Leveraging Social Media for Traffic

The last segment of this chapter navigates the shifting terrain of social media as a formidable traffic-generating mechanism. Social networks have matured into bustling centres of activity and interaction, giving a direct channel to your target audience. Here, we study the methods and best practices for harnessing social media successfully. From generating captivating content to establishing true relationships with your audience, the arena of social media has great possibilities for increasing traffic, boosting your brand presence, and maintaining a devoted following. Understanding the subtleties of social media traffic production is vital for utilising the immense potential it brings to the modern digital ecosystem.

Chapter Five

Understanding and Taking Care of Your Audience

5.1 Growing a Faithful Community

Successful digital marketing begins with establishing a loyal online community. Your target market is not merely a bunch of faceless customers; they are human individuals with distinct needs, desires, and issues. It's vital to communicate with your audience genuinely if you want to establish loyalty. Start by paying attention to their comments and concerns. Promote frank debate in forums, social media, and comment spaces. You may demonstrate your attention to their pleasure by answering immediately and sensitively.

Transparency and trust are also vital for loyalty. Share your brand's objectives and values, ensuring they complement those of your audience. This trust is further developed by maintaining consistency in your messaging and keeping your word. Recognize and appreciate your loyal community members, as their dedication to your brand will be increased by your actions.

5.2 Essentials of Email Marketing

Effective audience nurturing continues to depend significantly on email marketing. Your email list is a direct conduit of communication to the inboxes of your audience, making it a valuable tool for developing relationships and encouraging purchases. Start by organically building your email list while focusing on quality over quantity. Promote sign-ups by delivering eye-catching lead magnets, such as ebooks, webinars, or special bargains. Effective email marketing depends significantly on segmentation. Adapt your message to the requirements, habits, and demographics of distinct target groups. Personalised content touches customers on a deeper level. Create emails that are fun to read, are topical, and provide insights.

Your email marketing efforts may be simplified with automation. Create automated email sequences to nurture prospects over time and aid in converting them. A comprehensive email marketing approach not only develops your audience but also assists in converting them into dedicated customers.

5.3 Content Marketing's Strength

The cornerstone of producing valuable, shareable, and memorable experiences for your audience is content marketing. Create a content strategy that takes your audience's needs and interests into consideration. Publish interesting, amusing, or instructional content regularly, such as blog posts, videos, podcasts, and infographics.

Keep in mind that content marketing is not simply about advertising oneself. It's about delivering your audience true value. You may position yourself as a subject matter expert in your profession by fixing their concerns and treating their pain points. By enabling comments, shares, and conversations about your work, you may improve engagement.

Promote your work through several venues, such as social media, email, and partnerships with influencers or business titans. Analyse performance metrics to continually enhance your content strategy. Your content will help you create better ties with your audience over time, transforming casual users into devoted advocates.

5.4 Making Your Messaging Personal

In today's digital world, one-size-fits-all marketing messages are no longer effective. The trick to making your audience feel heard and valued is customization. Take advantage of data and technology to grasp the preferences, activities, and prior purchases of your audience. You may tailor your message to each person's individual needs and interests utilising this information.

More than just including the recipient's name in an email counts as customization. It comprises making targeted offers, content suggestions, and appropriate product recommendations. Implement dynamic content that rapidly reacts to user action to give a more exciting and personalised experience.

Additionally, the story is a great personalising tool. Create tales that connect to the experiences and ambitions of your audience to boost the relatability of your brand. By making your message more customised to each audience member, you may boost conversion rates, audience loyalty, and engagement.

Chapter 6

The Secrets of Sales Copywriting

6.1 Writing Convincing Sales Copy

Successful online marketing is founded on great sales copywriting. Understanding your target consumer, their challenges, and the remedies your product or service delivers is crucial to crafting persuasive sales copy. Start by coming up with an attention-grabbing title that speaks to a specific problem or need. To clearly and simply communicate the benefits of your service, underline how it answers the customer's concern. Use persuasive methods like stressing significant aspects, replying to criticism, and giving testimonials or reviews as social proof. Include a compelling call to action (CTA) that pushes the reader in the direction of the targeted activity, such as making a purchase, signing up for something, or seeking further information.

6.2 Telling Stories to Sell

The use of tales in sales copywriting is beneficial because it appeals to customers' emotions and helps them connect to your brand and goods on a deeper level. Tell anecdotes that will appeal to your target market about how your product has improved the lives of others. Create tales that stress the problem-solution dynamic by putting the reader in a familiar position before offering your response. Empathic storytelling enhances audience trust in your brand and raises the chance that they will take the desired action. By adding anecdotes to your sales pitch, you may build a strong and lasting message that separates you from the competition.

6.3.2 Split-testing Your Copy

The most effective technique to optimise your sales copy is through A/B testing. It comprises making two (or more) versions of your text with slight modifications, putting them through a series of tests to discover which performs better, and documenting the findings. Start by determining which specific components, such as headlines, CTA buttons, or product descriptions, you want to test. To split your audience and measure critical metrics like conversion rates, click-through rates, and bounce rates, employ A/B testing tools and platforms. Analyse the results frequently and make copy edits based on data-driven insights. A/B testing makes sure that your sales copy improves and gets better over time, resulting in increased conversions and a larger return on investment.

6.4 Resources and Tools for Copywriting

Utilising the diversity of tools and resources at your disposal is vital if you want to achieve in the area of sales copywriting. Start by employing research tools to better appreciate the preferences, challenges, and behaviours of your target audience. The most relevant and high-converting keywords for your work may be picked with the aid of keyword research tools. Email marketing platforms and content management systems (CMS) give templates and automated options for effectively spreading your message. Tools for grammar and proofreading are vital for making sure your work is perfect and well-presented. Take into consideration things like copywriting clubs, books, and courses as well if you want to stay up with industry advances and maintain your talents fresh. Investing in these tools and sources can substantially enhance your copywriting talents and help your internet marketing activities succeed.

Chapter Seven

Improving Conversion Rates

7.1 Conversions as a Science

Conversion rate optimization is a talent that is fundamental to all successful online business initiatives. It's a science that goes considerably beyond mere practice to grasp user psychology and behaviour. Conversion optimization is to understand the subtleties of why people sometimes abandon a website without accomplishing the specified activity. Businesses obtain insights into the preferences, issues, and decision-making processes of their target audience through data analysis and continuing development. They can build techniques that speak to the wants of their audience owing to this scientific approach, which finally results in better conversion rates.

7.2 Multivariate and Split Testing

Split testing and multivariate testing are key strategies in the endeavour to boost conversion rates. Split testing means producing numerous revisions of a website, email, or advertising and sending various audiences to each variant. Businesses may discover which components—be they headlines, call-to-action buttons, visuals, or copy—have the biggest effect on conversion by carefully examining the performance data of numerous versions. Multivariate testing takes one step further by exploring the relationships and effects of alternative configurations of these variables on conversion rates. These testing procedures give the factual evidence necessary to make data-driven decisions and refine marketing tactics for the greatest results.

7.3 Aiming to Improve User Experience

Delivering an outstanding user experience is a critical component of conversion rate optimization; it goes beyond making tiny modifications to enhance conversions. Visitor conversion rates are greater on websites and apps that are fluid and simple to use. Businesses must focus on issues like website load speed, mobile responsiveness, uncomplicated navigation, and clear value proposition communication to enhance user experience. Businesses may develop an environment that fosters increased conversion rates by making sure that visitors can easily locate what they're seeking and have a favourable experience with the brand.

7.4 Improving Conversion Rates

The ultimate purpose of conversion rate optimization is to enhance your conversion rate. This needs a complete approach that blends the insights obtained through multivariate testing, split testing, and user experience enhancements. It involves ongoing examination and gradual improvements to numerous components of your online presence, from landing pages and product descriptions to checkout processes and customer service. To enhance conversion rates, customization and targeting are also necessary. You may drastically enhance the possibility of conversion by concentrating your marketing efforts on select customer groups and producing appropriate messages and offers for them. Remember that the route to optimization is one-way and requires steadiness, adaptability, and a clear commitment to offering value to your audience.

Chapter Eight

The Role of Value Ladders

8.1 Building Your Value Ladder

In the realm of Internet marketing, the notion of a value ladder is a vital component for the continuous development and profitability of your organisation. Your value ladder is simply a series of offers and goods that increase in value and price, responding to the varied wants and budgets of your clients. At the base of the ladder, you have your entry-level or low-cost offerings, generally aimed to attract a wide audience. As clients scale this ladder, they meet higher-priced and more valuable items.

The process of constructing your value ladder starts with a comprehensive knowledge of your target audience's requirements, desires, and pain areas. By connecting each rung of your ladder with these insights, you can develop engaging offers that appeal to your clients at each point of their journey. Start with a low-cost or free offer to grab leads and take them into your ecosystem. As you advance, try delivering mid-tier items or services that give greater value and answers to particular challenges. Finally, at the top of the ladder, display your premium options, which provide the most complete solutions and advantages.

8.2 Upselling and Cross-Selling Strategies

Once you have created your value ladder, the skill of upselling and cross-selling comes into play. Upselling entails enticing clients to upgrade to a higher-priced product or bundle with more value. Cross-selling, on the other hand, promotes complementing items or services that improve the customer's entire experience.

Effective upselling and cross-selling methods demand a thorough awareness of your customer's preferences and wants. By integrating data and consumer behaviour analytics, you can tailor your suggestions and make them more relevant. Additionally, timing is key. Implement upsell and cross-sell offers at crucial touchpoints, such as during the checkout process or after a consumer has completed a purchase. When performed successfully, these techniques not only boost income per client but also promote customer happiness by delivering personalised solutions.

8.3 Customer Lifetime Value

Understanding and maximising Customer Lifetime Value (CLV) is a vital aspect of a successful value ladder strategy. CLV indicates the overall income a client earns during their entire association with your organisation. To calculate CLV effectively, consider parameters such as purchase frequency, average order value, and retention rate.

By raising CLV, you optimise the return on your marketing effort. This may be done by creating outstanding customer experiences, cultivating loyalty via rewards programs, and consistently introducing higher-value items or services to your current customer base. Remember that nurturing and maintaining current customers frequently costs less than gaining new ones, making CLV a vital indicator for sustainable development.

8.4 Creating Raving Fans

At the core of a well-constructed value ladder lies the objective of developing raving fans—loyal consumers who not only buy from you frequently but also become champions for your company. These passionate fans not only contribute considerably to your CLV but also play a critical role in generating new clients via word-of-mouth marketing.

To generate enthusiastic fans, emphasise excellent customer experiences and continually surpass their expectations. Engage with your consumers via tailored messages, ask and act on their feedback, and reward their loyalty. Encourage user-generated material and testimonials to illustrate the good experiences of your consumers, developing trust and credibility within your niche.

Chapter Nine

Traffic Temperature and Segmentation

9.1 Recognizing the temperature of the traffic

Understanding the notion of traffic temperature is vital in the continuously changing world of internet marketing. The amount of familiarity and interest that visitors have when they visit your website or interact with your marketing materials is referred to as the "traffic temperature." This principle is vital to knowing how to effectively engage and convert your audience. The three primary temperatures of traffic are cold, warm, and hot.

People who have had little to no prior exposure to your brand or merchandise are referred to as "cold traffic." They have the lowest degree of awareness and are strangers to your brand. Warm traffic is made up of visitors who have connected with your content in some manner, such as by subscribing to your newsletter or following you on social media. Hot traffic is made up of folks who are presently your customers or who have shown a lot of interest in what you have to offer.

9.2 Identifying Audience Subgroups

The core of personalised marketing is segmentation, which comprises dividing your audience according to similar features, behaviours, or interests. You may adapt your marketing efforts to each group's specific needs and preferences by segmenting your audience. By adopting this strategy, you can develop offers and content that are more engaging and relevant, which ultimately leads to increased conversion rates and happier consumers.

A range of characteristics, similar to demographics, psychographics, purchase history, and degree of participation, may be utilised to segment audiences efficiently. To make sure that your marketing efforts are successful with the target audience, each group needs to be carefully defined and explained. You may build techniques that satisfy their specific needs and expectations by being aware that diverse segments might encounter differing traffic temperatures.

9.3 Creating Customised Marketing Messages

The essential next step is to adjust your marketing message to appeal to each group once you have located and segmented your audience. In the digital environment, one-size-fits-all tactics rarely give the greatest results. Your message should instead be about the particular demands, challenges, and interests of each sector.

Your communications for cold traffic should focus on promoting your company and creating awareness. For growing this audience, instructional content and value-driven offerings are valuable tools. More customised content boosts the trust and engagement of warm traffic. Emphasising the distinctive aspects of your products or services may be incredibly convincing. Conversely, hot traffic may merely require direct offers and incentives to convert or make additional sales.

9.4 Dynamic marketing efforts

Dynamic marketing tactics take advantage of the fluidity of online interactions and changes in audience preferences and habits. You may design campaigns that respond instantaneously to user interactions by employing automation technology and data. These commercials' primary aspects include dynamic content, personalised recommendations, and behavioural triggers.

When utilised in combination with targeted audiences and traffic temperature knowledge, dynamic marketing is incredibly successful. It helps you to send targeted messages and offers at the appropriate moment, improving the possibility of conversion. Dynamic campaigns may dramatically increase your marketing performance and overall customer experience, whether it be through abandoned cart emails, targeted product suggestions, or time-sensitive promos.

The answer to optimising your marketing efforts in the digital arena is to have a clear knowledge of traffic temperature and segmentation. You may design a marketing strategy that accurately and efficiently engages, converts, and retains customers by understanding the temperature of your audience, segmenting them effectively, tailoring your messaging, and putting dynamic campaigns into action.

Chapter Ten

The Strength of Follow-Up Funnels

10.1 The Value of Following Up

The significance of follow-up cannot be overstated in the context of online marketing and sales. It is typically the determining aspect of converting potential leads into paying customers. When a visitor engages with your website or reads your content, they may not be prepared to purchase right now. Follow-up sequences address this gap by developing prospects over time, building a feeling of trust, and retaining brand awareness. The critical importance that follow-up sequences perform in the sales process is studied in this chapter, with a concentration on how they could turn fleeting curiosity into lasting customer relationships.

10.2 Automating the Follow-Up Process

Successful online firms pride themselves on their efficiency, and automating follow-up sequences is a vital element of doing so. By automating this process, you can focus on other critical parts of your organisation while still ensuring that your leads receive timely and appropriate messages without human intervention. Automation streamlines your follow-up efforts, removing human mistakes and maintaining consistency in communication, whether it's sending out welcome emails, product recommendations, or targeted promotions based on user behaviour. The strategies, tactics, and best practices for developing and operating automated follow-up funnels are addressed in this section.

10.3 Email Chains That Work

Due to its versatility and success, email marketing continues to be a crucial component of follow-up funnels. Understanding your audience's needs, segmenting your contacts, and offering valuable information that resonates are all critical components of building compelling email sequences. This section describes the structure of great email sequences, including how to design attractive subject lines, arrange emails for best impact, and utilise customisation to build a tighter relationship with subscribers. In addition, we go over how to stay clear of classic errors and enhance email sequences for improved open rates, click-through rates, and conversions.

10.4 Scaling Your Following-Up Funnels

Your follow-up channels should increase together with your online firm. To keep the quality and relevance of your follow-up sequences while growing these funnels, careful planning and execution are essential. This section analyses the ways to expand your follow-up funnels effectively, including building your email list, audience segmentation for more targeted messaging, and the usage of cutting-edge automation technologies. We also go over the relevance of data analysis and insight collection to continually upgrade your follow-up sequences and make sure they remain in line with your evolving corporate goals.

Chapter Eleven

Webinar Funnels' Secrets

A formidable device in the domain of online marketing and sales is the webinar. We'll look into the numerous sides of webinar funnels in this chapter, including their usage as a sales tool, ways for developing interesting presentations, tactics for improving webinar funnels, and recommendations for organising efficient webinar events.

11.1 Using webinars for sales

When utilised appropriately, webinars can be a highly powerful sales tool. They allow you a place for in-depth contact with your audience, helping you to showcase the advantages of your products or services. With the usage of webinars, you may grow your authority in your industry, promote trust, and finally enhance conversions. Webinars may effectively move prospects through your sales funnel by delivering instructional content and addressing your audience's pain concerns.

11.2 Designing Interesting Webinars

The talent-generating riveting webinars need precise planning and execution. Start by getting acquainted with the expectations and preferences of your target audience. Create an interesting tale that speaks to them. Apply narrative tactics to your information to make it memorable and meaningful. Use visuals to promote knowledge and hold viewers' attention, such as slides and graphics. Additionally, a sense of connection is generated and participants are kept engaged by the effective use of interactive components like surveys and Q&A sessions.

11.3 Optimising the webinar funnel

For your webinar to be as effective as possible, it must be optimised. Optimise your registration process first. Sign-up rates may be boosted by employing persuasive information and simple, short landing pages. Equally vital is pre-webinar communication, which helps to persuade guests to register and generate enthusiasm. Implement strategies to decrease drop-offs during the webinar, such as sustaining a rapid pace, offering useful content throughout, and resolving concerns. The funnel is finished by post-webinar follow-up, which may include email sequences and tailored offers. This guarantees that leads are nurtured and converted.

11.4 Organising Webinars That Are Successful

A webinar's success hinges on meticulous planning and execution. Start by picking the finest webinar platform that supports your aims. To ensure a flawless delivery, rehearse your presentation. On the day of the event, get there early to welcome early attendees and deal with any technical difficulties. Engage your audience and offer them a feeling of significance and respect. Employing surveys, chat, and live Q&A sessions, boosts engagement. Finally, sum up the most essential elements from the webinar, reaffirm your offer, and give clear next steps, including how to acquire your product or service.

Chapter Twelve

Building Effective Membership Sites

12.1 Membership Websites as a Source of Income

The landscape of online business has witnessed the growth of membership sites as a solid and sustainable revenue stream. In exchange for recurring membership charges, some platforms give premium services, community involvement, or unique content. Membership websites appeal to both company owners and content providers owing to their constant income and devoted consumer base. The key to success in this industry is to determine your target market and audience, know their wants, and give value that justifies the faithful membership of your clients.

12.2 Producing Useful Content for Membership

Any membership website's content is what drives it. You must consistently deliver high-quality, original information that appeals to your members' interests and issues to keep them engaged and subscribed. The format of this content could vary, including articles, videos, webinars, and downloadable resources. Relevance, however, is the key factor. Your information should fulfil your members' expectations and offer them answers or insights they can't obtain elsewhere. Maintaining your membership site's value proposition needs effective content planning, scheduling, and production techniques.

12.3 Techniques for Retaining Members

The key to a successful membership site is member retention. High turnover rates may severely diminish your revenue and risk the viability of your firm over the long term. Consequently, it is vital to adopt member retention techniques. Personalization is crucial to retention methods. A sense of community and value is established by customising content and engagement experiences to unique member choices and activities. Additionally, retaining members' pleasure and loyalty demands a proactive approach to communication, regular feedback collection, and rapid issue resolution. Rewards like loyalty systems, invitation-only gatherings, or levels of membership may assist in enhancing retention.

12.4 Scaling Your Membership Business

Scalability becomes a crucial problem when your membership site grows in popularity.

Scaling entails extending your client base and revenue without also expanding your workload or available resources. Consider broadening your content offerings or widening your speciality to attract a broader audience to develop effectively. Processes for recruiting new members and onboarding them may be expedited by adopting marketing automation technologies. Your reach may be boosted and your membership site might reach new audiences through partnerships and collaborations within your field. Additionally, if you invest in a solid infrastructure and support systems, your website will be able to handle larger traffic while still offering top-notch service as your membership organisation increases.

It needs a methodical approach to establish a high-performing membership site that involves planning for scalability, content development, and retention activities. You may establish a profitable membership site that not only earns cash but also nourishes a loyal and involved community of subscribers by continually delivering value to your customers, grasping their wants, and enhancing your tactics.

Chapter Thirteen

The Digital Commerce Strategies Toolbox

Success in internet marketing relies on the smart use of a multitude of tools and approaches in today's digital world. This chapter discusses the fundamental instruments in the Digital Commerce Strategies
arsenal, each of which has a special purpose in the pursuit of online excellence.

13.1 Important Online Marketing Resources

One needs to employ a robust armoury of tools to navigate through the complexity of the digital world. These encompass a wide spectrum, including social media management tools, email marketing platforms, and website builders and content management systems. It is crucial to pick suitable tools depending on your business's objectives. The efficiency of marketers is considerably boosted by the usage of tools like graphic design software, social media schedulers, and SEO keyword research platforms.

13.2 Analytics and tracking

The ability to examine and analyse performance indicators is vital in the domain of online marketing. Businesses have access to analytical analytics tools like Google Analytics and Facebook Insights that help them understand more about user behaviour, traffic sources, and conversion rates. This data-driven technique facilitates continuing marketing plan refinement. monitoring pixels and conversion monitoring increase measurement accuracy of campaign outcomes and serve as the cornerstone for informed decision-making.

13.3 Workflow and automation

In the age of digital business, the saying "time is money" is particularly pertinent. Process streamlining, efficiency enhancement, and time savings are all advantages of automation technology and workflow solutions. Personalised, timely, and targeted communications may be produced utilising marketing automation technologies like HubSpot and email marketing automation platforms like MailChimp. Workflow automation tools like Zapier make it easy to link multiple apps and platforms, which reduces human effort and boosts productivity.

13.4 Delegation and Outsourcing

Knowing when and how to divide obligations is a skill of major value in the search for sustainable development. The burden of internal staff members may be decreased, and specialised experience may be brought to the table, by outsourcing to specialists in sectors like content production, web development, or SEO. Task delegation is made simpler with the use of virtual assistants and project management software, which encourages a flexible and adaptive work environment. The ability to delegate jobs to experienced employees frees up firm executives' time to focus on strategic challenges and developing their operations.

Chapter Fourteen

Scaling Your Online Empire

14.1 Growth Techniques and Scaling

The important change from a small-scale firm to a big business needs a disciplined approach to growth to develop an online empire. The road map for negotiating this transformation is growth strategies. Adopting a clear growth strategy entails having a complete grasp of your target market, the competition, and market trends. Market penetration, product creation, market development, and diversification are common methods, but they may vary. Each strategy has individual aims and risk profiles, demanding cautious selection depending on the particular requirements of your firm. It's vital to examine the consequences of your preferred technique on resources, infrastructure, and organisational abilities to develop sustainably.

14.2 Increasing Your Product Offering

A major component of establishing your online empire is extending your product offering. By delivering additional value to your clients, variety within your products not only appeals to a larger client group but also enhances customer retention. This increase, however, needs to be properly planned. It comprises market research, competition analysis, and a deep grasp of the likes and needs of your present customer base. The brand's identity should be preserved and the customers' expectations for quality and consistency should be satisfied by the new products or services. A successful increase in product variety also demands a sensible strategy for pricing, marketing, and customer support for these extra items.

14.3 Global Development

While expanding into international markets provides substantial growth potential, it also adds complexity and risk. Considerations for growing overseas include cultural peculiarities, legal and regulatory frameworks, shifting currencies, and logistics. To locate the most promising locations and alter your products or services to satisfy the individual demands of each market, rigorous market research is important. Establishing local subsidiaries or partnerships could help an entry go more smoothly. Furthermore, for obtaining momentum and creating trust in foreign markets, good communication and localization of your brand message are crucial. Your online empire may fly to new heights with a well-thought-out overseas development plan, but it demands meticulous preparation and execution.

14.4 Maintaining Agility in a Changing Environment

The digital world is dynamic and continually evolving. Agility is vital for sustaining and increasing your online company. Maintaining agility demands regular study of market trends, consumer trends, and technology changes. A competitive advantage may be acquired by reacting to new technologies like blockchain and artificial intelligence. Maintaining a flexible organisational structure that supports innovation and rapid decision-making is also vital. Adopt an experimental approach and be prepared to alter direction if necessary. Staying adaptable also entails building resilience into your business plan to prepare for unforeseen disruptions like economic downturns or global catastrophes. The success of your online empire will rely on your skill to adapt, pivot, and innovate in this continuously evolving environment.

Chapter Fithteen

Leaving a Legacy and Volunteering

15.1 Making a Sustainable Business

The notion of legacy in today's changing digital world extends beyond monetary wealth and professional achievement. It entails establishing a sustainable firm that will survive for many years. Such a corporation demands rigorous planning, moral conduct, and a determination to longevity. Sustainability incorporates social and environmental responsibility in addition to financial achievement. Businesses that utilise environmentally friendly strategies not only lower their carbon footprint but also win over an increasing market of environmentally informed clients. Additionally, providing a supportive work atmosphere and investing money in employee health may have a huge influence on your company's long-term success. A long legacy is founded on a sustainable firm that achieves a balance between profits and ambitions.

15.2 Charity and assisting others

An excellent approach to giving back to society and creating an impact that lasts is through philanthropy. You have the option to give cash to excellent organisations and enhance the lives of others while your business develops. Successful philanthropy must be carefully thought out and by your views and aims. Giving back, whether by monetary donations, volunteer work, or partnerships with charitable organisations, may promote goodwill, enhance the image of your company, and have a favourable knock-on influence within your community and beyond. In addition to being a benevolent act, generosity is a purposeful choice to leave a lasting legacy that goes beyond monetary benefit.

15.3 Leaving a Long-Term Impression

Beyond the business sphere, creating a lasting impact encompasses your influence and the lives you touch. By offering relevant knowledge and lessons acquired from your experience to prospective entrepreneurs, you may coach and inspire them. Your impact may also be felt through thought leadership and innovation, which will progress both your industry and society at large. Additionally, developing trusted ties with colleagues, partners, and customers may create a long-lasting network of support. Understanding the power of your influence and leveraging it to your advantage may help you create a lasting impression.

15.4 The Legacy of Digital Commerce Strategies

The Digital Commerce Strategies
ideology emphasises building a community of like-minded people who are devoted to moral and efficient internet marketing techniques in addition to attaining individual success. This legacy is founded on the ideals of transparency, value creation, and devotion to the success of others. As you put the concepts and methods from this book into practice, you become a part of its legacy and contribute to the drive to raise the standard for online business. Your journey, your triumphs, and your community engagement become key aspects of Digital Commerce Strategies
' continuing tale. Your legacy in this context is evidence of the long-lasting value of shared knowledge and moral entrepreneurship.

Conclusion

We've been on a revolutionary trip through the difficulties of internet marketing and corporate development due to "Digital Commerce Strategies." We've looked at the fundamental notions that drive success in the online world, comprehended the finer details of developing enticing products, and mastered the complexities of traffic generation and sales funnels. We've found how vital it is to increase our audience, generate interesting content, and enhance conversion rates. We've learnt the significance of sustainability, charity, and creating a lasting mark along the route.

It's vital to bear in mind that "Digital Commerce Strategies" is more than merely a book as we near the end of our voyage it's a roadmap for leaving a lasting legacy. It serves as a timely reminder that success in the digital arena is not just about collecting money, but also about making a lasting influence on society. It's about developing enterprises that survive, giving back to society, and leaving a legacy that goes beyond financial success.

We enrich our businesses while also creating a bigger, shared legacy—the Digital Commerce Strategies legacy—by embracing the virtues of sustainability, generosity, and long-lasting effect. This legacy is marked by a devotion to moral entrepreneurship, knowledge sharing, and assisting others to accomplish their dreams in the digital world.

You contribute to this history when you absorb these concepts and employ them in your online endeavours. Your experiences, successes, and contributions are woven into the fabric of Digital Commerce Strategies, impacting the evolution of online commerce for future generations.

So, armed with the information you've learned and your aim and conviction, move forth. Create sustainable companies, give freely to the community, and leave a lasting effect. Your legacy in the digital realm will be one of quality, honesty, and long-lasting success. We appreciate you joining the Digital Commerce Strategies community. We wish you success on your trip and offer you the delight of leaving a lasting imprint.